GRACE
BEFORE PLOUGHING

THE WORKS OF JOHN MASEFIELD

PLAYS

The Faithful
Good Friday
Tristan and Isolt
Easter
Melloney Holtspur

A King's Daughter
The Trial of Jesus
The Tragedy of Nan
The Coming of Christ
End and Beginning

POETRY

Dauber
The Daffodil Fields
Philip the King
Lollingdon Downs
A Poem and Two Plays
Reynard the Fox
Enslaved
Right Royal
Selected Poems (new edition)
King Cole
Old Raiger and Other Verse

Poems (collected)
Midsummer Night
Minnie Maylow's Story
A Tale of Troy
A Letter from Pontus
Gautama the Enlightened
Wonderings
Natalie Maisie and Pavilastukay
On the Hill
The Bluebells and Other Verse

FICTION

Sard Harker
Odtaa
The Midnight Folk
The Hawbucks
The Bird of Dawning
The Taking of the Gry
The Box of Delights

Victorious Troy
Eggs and Baker
The Square Peg
Dead Ned
Live and Kicking Ned
Basilissa
Conquer

GENERAL

Gallipoli
The Old Front Line
St George and the Dragon
The Battle of the Somme
Recent Prose
With the Living Voice
The Wanderer of Liverpool
Poetry: A Lecture
So Long to Learn
Grace Before Ploughing

The Conway
The Nine Days Wonder
In the Mill
New Chum
Thanks Before Going and A
    Macbeth Production
A Book of Both Sorts
A Book of Prose Selections
William Shakespeare

JOHN MASEFIELD

Grace Before Ploughing

Fragments of Autobiography

The Macmillan Company

NEW YORK

Library of Congress Catalog Card Number: 66-21163

FIRST AMERICAN PRINTING

The Macmillan Company, New York

Printed in the United States of America

CONTENTS

v

Prologue

Once, looking north, the daisied meadow filled
With multitude, by miracle, unwilled;
Men, of no mortals born,
Splendid as flowers, many as the corn,
Marching with banners to a tune that thrilled.

I saw, I heard, I marvelled; but they ceast . . .
Naught but the meadow-grass was north and east,
I cried, 'O come again . . .
You singing men out-numbering the rain
And take me, too, to conquest or to feast.'

I trod the rocky road of no reply.
They trod a way unseen by mortal eye,
To some immortal end,
With life for bread, with ecstasy for friend,
Their very substance that which cannot die.

Still, in my heart, that marching music rings,
Those faces glow of men whose wills were wings.
Powers, by beauty shriven,
A spark of immortality has given
An immortality to mortal things.

I

The Linked Paradises

FOR some years, like many children, I lived in Paradise, or, rather, like a specially lucky child in two Paradises linked together by a country of exceeding beauty and strangeness.

In the one extreme, I was told that the ancient joy of Britons, the plant woad, grew; and in the other extreme there was The Wonder, where a hill moved for three days screaming as though it hurt.

Other reasons than this made me prefer the former: I did not much want to stain myself blue if the blue were a fast dye impossible to change, but the less a landscape screamed, I thought, the better.

The linked Paradises are parted from each other by some hilly miles of rural England and by two of the English rivers. For some blissful years I knew them both as only a child can know a country. No child can have a great range, but he knows his mile, or at most two miles, better than the grown-up knows his parish and has (besides) a sufficient sense of the worth of the people in it.

The two places when put together would be but small. The larger one is about two miles long by rather less in breadth, in and near the small market town of Ledbury in Herefordshire. The other is a tiny strip of Bredon Hill and the River Avon in Worcestershire.

The two scenes are linked as one in glad memory of happiness. They are parted from the sight of each other by the line of the Malvern Hills, of which the Herefordshire Beacon keeps Bredon Hill from any possible sight of Ledbury, though in my young days the people at the Beacon could see on any clear day the great spire of Ledbury Church; and then, turning round, could see Bredon, and sometimes even also see the Boundary Stone and the little tower above it.

The distance between the two extreme points of the church below Bredon Hill top and the Roman camp at Wall Hills cannot be more than twenty miles, as the crow flies. The difference between the inhabitants is very great (or ever seemed to me to be so), as though the tribes that composed the inhabitants were of a different stock altogether, the one not always well disposed to the other.

My earliest memories are of these two places and of spots very near to them. My early memories are therefore of fertile orchards full of fruit; of hills much marked with old tribal settlements; of rivers prone to flood, of many ancient buildings; and peopled by most kind folk who yet kept alive, deep in their hearts, a memory of the Civil War 'against Oliver'.

2

Ledbury

THE little market town of Ledbury in Herefordshire has one long street crossed by two other lesser streets, both of which were watered by never-failing springs that rise in the hills near by.

It has a fine church, with notable work by the men of the Middle Ages; the belfry (apart from the church, as in several other churches on the Welsh border) has a fair peal of bells and a fine spire.

In the course of time I came to know the town and its place under some wooded hills very well, but never knew any of it so well as the little area that I knew first in my first six and a half years. In those first years it was touched with a beauty and a glory that no later time could give. In this book I hope to set down something of what it seemed to me. I write now late in life, from a memory that has forgotten much, but what memory still exists is vivid beyond all other memories, and centres upon what *I* first saw in my home, there, in the last house on the west of the Hereford Road by which men then went to the station. There has been much building on that road since then, but the fields then stretched from our fence to the Hereford Road without a house.

Somewhere in that house I began to notice and remember things, though I am not sure that I was born there. I have some reason to suppose that I was not born there, but I leave that to others. Somewhere in that house I began to look upon what of Victorian England could be seen there.

I suppose that I first looked out of its western windows on an orchard, a more distant field, a long clump of elms with a great rookery in its forty or fifty trees, a canal that flowed, as I thought, from Paradise to Heaven, though some have doubted this, and then miles of woodland that barred much of the distant view.

In the fields beyond the canal, in wet weather, a wide reddish smudge would appear, which I was told was the floods. In ordinary seasons I looked beyond these fields to a wooded hill, and to the left, or south, of this hill to a more distant, less wooded hill, which I was told was Marcle, and that Marcle was where The Wonder was.

Marcle and some of its wonder was to be shown to me long afterwards. The place has known some strangeness that has left its marks. I found these impressive, but they are out of my subject here.

Of Marcle, I will only say here, that when it was going to rain it looked very clear, and in the clearness a new land appeared beyond it.

I was told that the new land was Wales, and that these were the Black Hills.

I did not like the sound of the Black Hills, nor what was told to me of Wales and the Welsh. I learned at a very early age something of the feeling of the border, where the two races met but did not much mingle. The English of the border did not approve of the Welsh; and the Welsh returned the prejudice. The feeling was shared by young and old: the young caught the infection without knowing that it was an infection. I looked at that shadowy land like a dim cloud on the horizon, and knew from my elders that that was Wales, the land of the Welsh, who were not the English but a foreign race, with whom our natives disagreed.

I cannot tell when I first knew of the disagreement but something of it was imparted to me in my first years. I knew, for instance, that an Englishman would begin the trouble by a swift recognition of the Welshman and the familiar greeting:

'O, Effan Chones, who trowned the tuck? Who stole the monkey, look you?'

To this the Welshman would answer in general terms:

'An Englissman; he is a plight on Cot's earth, look you.'

But for the earliest years of my life I was less aware of this feeling against the Welsh than of a Civil War feeling, that Hereford and the Welsh had stood for the King, and that across the Severn to the east from us were others who had taken another side. I was to hear much about that business in my early youth, for its passions still ran high.

For the moment I will say only that my first impressions were of a westward view over some orchards of fertile Hereford. I could look from the windows of my home to a wooded distance, beneath which a little river, the Leddon, ran much subject to floods in thaws and wet weather.

Much nearer to me, in a middle distance of about 200 yards, there stretched visibly one of the wonders of the world, the Gloucester and Hereford Canal, which made a straight course north at that point for a marvellous mile or two.

Later, I was to see ships famous in the history of such things, the marvellous Scotch clippers, Irish masterpieces, and English triumphs. But what were these to the barges that entranced a little boy; barges that were sailing from Paradise to Heaven, carrying hearts of gold and cargoes of wonder, and always, always, returning a salute, even at a distance?

I must now say a little about the town of Ledbury, as I saw it in those first years; I lived on its northern fringe and did not go much into the town itself. My memory of it, as it then was, is that some of its eastern sidewalks were paved with cobblestones of small sizes that made most painful going to little feet. I knew, too, that at the Bye Street I might see and hear the timber wagons coming in from some of the woods with tree trunks. Somewhere in the west a lot of timber was being cut, and brought into the Homend there. I know not where it went later, but the timber-carters were fine, hearty fellows, who made a point of entering the market place with a cracking of whips. The whips themselves were rather short in the handle and long and heavy in the plaited lash. I do not suppose for a moment that the horses were ever beaten by such men, but the cracking of the whips was like small-arms fire. The men made a practice of walking beside their teams as they entered the market place, and as warnings to those in the main street they cracked their whips with a skill and noise that encouraged their teams, and gave 'audible warning of their approach'. The skill of the whip-crackers was wonderful. After a visit to the spot, I would make myself a whip with a stick from the woodshed and a piece of string, and try unavailingly to make that fiery crackle that gave such life to the town. It may be that timber

6

coming into the town is no longer drawn by horses, but by engines of some sort. Human skill is no doubt still displayed there, but no longer the inspiriting sight of men and horses at one; the men urging the teams by cheer and whip-crack, and the horses responding to the cheer, with their great souls greatly exhorted and the great trees brought round the bend.

Just opposite the entrance to Bye Street, where the whips so gunnily cracked, was the old seventeenth-century Market Place and the entrance to the Church Lane. In the Lane at that time were some tanneries with a peculiar stench, somehow considered wholesome. The little lane was dark and overhung with buildings; people said that many had died of the plague there and that Prince Rupert had charged up the lane at the Battle of Ledbury. Some said that he had charged down it, but my own feeling now is that no horse could have charged either up or down it. One wheelbarrow across the gangway would have blocked it as a thoroughfare.

The lane led directly into the churchyard to which I had not, at that early age, been forced to attend.

On the Ross Road there was a busy forge, where we often lingered to see horses shod. Near to this was the nearest canal lock to which we had easy access. These two places gave me as a little child the liveliest interest in men's skill and power. The taming of the horse and the compelling of water to man's service remain marvels of man's advance and range. They have been great steps upon his way.

I think that these few words tell all that I knew, liked, and thought much of in Ledbury itself. I cannot have been much in the town in my first years. My daily walks and my chief interests were in the roads, fields and scenes close to my home in the country within a mile west, north and east from our gate; and in the direction of Hereford, to the west, of Bosbury to the north and of Malvern to the east.

3

October Fair

IN that beginning of my life, I knew little of Ledbury as a seaport or as a market-town. I knew very little of it save as the scene of a great yearly marvel called the October Fair, of which I thought with hope and rapture all the year round. On that great day in early October there was joyous holiday. It was a hiring fair, where men sought employment for the coming year, and the broad main street was glad with the sports of the fair: swings, merry-go-rounds, and coconut shies. It was busy also with the work of the fair: the sale of beasts of many kinds, which came there looking their smartest, to be judged and tried, in pens in the crowded street in the tumult of noise that made the fair so wonderful.

The sideshows: swings, merry-go-rounds, rifle booths, and so forth, kept to the west side; the pens of the beasts were east from there. In any clear space men tried the paces of the horses for sale. Under the market building, and in a paven space just south from it, there were egg and cheese and butter sellers, and the cheap-jacks, with their patter, and their piles of crockery.

Those days were long before the days of the modern road. For the October Fair, the roads were decked in ways now seldom seen. In the road, and between paving-stones on the sidewalks, men placed wonderful painted zinnias

9

on wooden sticks. The effect upon children was astonishing: nothing more beautiful could surely be in the world.

By daylight the town began to fill up with those who had come for the fair. Trains brought many people who could be recognized as Welsh, not by their speech alone, nor by their costume, for they wore no national costume, but by their radical difference of race. At a very early age, the young Anglo-Saxon will recognize a departure from his own racial type. But early in the day, the strangers would not be noticed with insult; the day's end heard the mocks and saw the conflicts.

To a little boy, the aspect of the Market Place was one of entrancing interest, noise and glad excitement. There was a mingling of rude music, song, and cries of cheer; cheapjacks were calling their goods, raising loud laughter, or smashing plates when bidders would not bargain for them. Mechanical music came from the merry-go-rounds, and from mouth-organs played by those in the swings. All those who had goods to sell spoke in their wares' praise.

All the beasts and fowls from local farms, brought there for sale, added their cries and calls. Horses were being tried for short distances; pigs and sheep were complaining in their pens; and men were praising their wares or their beasts at the tops of their voices.

In a fine October morning the scene had great beauty. The wide open space between well-built, prosperous-looking houses, often remarkable for their beauty and proportion; the great enjoyment of the crowd, their good temper and kindliness; the music giving grace to all that life; all these things combined to make the scene one of power upon the heart. Usually, too, there were mummers, in their traditional costume.

Later in the day, perhaps, the scene was less attractive. The beasts in the pens perhaps would be gone and the scene would lose the appearance of the fair, and become more a place of amusement. Various amusements started when the business had ended: a boxing booth would open for the young men eager to try their skill; others would be tempted to show their strength, by hitting a pestle with a mallet. The mallet in itself was a good weight. If it struck the pestle fairly, there would come a great clatter and the weight moved by the blow would be visibly registered. This was ever a favourite sport with the young men.

Temptations to show their skill or strength were such as few young men resisted. They would be tempted to have three shies for a penny at old Aunt Sally, and seeing that every time you hit you would get a good cigar. You could also roll, bowl or pitch sticks or balls at marks or coconuts.

The child who could not take part in the contest, could still watch the effort.

I know now that in those early October Fairs there were booths with little theatrical groups playing (with much skill) old plays of an earlier time. I grieve that I never saw these.

To this day, I remember vividly the young men in the high swings putting their weights on the rope that gave them their delight; the figure of the St George of a crew of mummers; the voices and the smashers of crockery of the cheap-jacks and all the marvel of the kindly happy people now all dead, save the little boy who once was with them, marvelling at the zinnias.

As it was a hiring fair, one saw the country crafts offering their skills: the shepherds, carters or cattlemen, and many indoor and outdoor workers who sought new masters for the coming year.

The Fair Days were days of wonder. I know now that there were things that I now shall never have the chance of seeing: two teams of mummers, with their tales of wonder, some dancers, some singers, all of these men of skill now vanished; and perhaps the last performers of famous plays about the Murder in the Red Barn, or Shaw the Life-Guardsman. All the joy of that old England was there every year, and I could have known it, and did not know it.

4

Malvern

About four miles from Ledbury, the road climbs a steep hill above which the main body of the Herefordshire Beacon rises. The steep hill was called Chance's Pitch and at that time refreshed the traveller with a gushing brook. It was famed in story (and terrified many children with the story), for it was said that in some fearful storm a coach and four went off the road there, in the snow, and came to death and disaster. I know not when this was, but supposed (wrongly) that this was the Pitch that Chance got or the Chance that Pitch got.

I knew it first from going up it and hearing the tale, on what was my first conscious visit to the Herefordshire Beacon, the nearest of the Malvern hills to us.

I was driven there, with a grown-up guest. At Chance's Pitch, I heard the story of the disaster to the coach, with the poetical addition that the ghosts of the killed coachman and guard still haunted the place to warn people of the danger. I have never quite forgotten that story.

When we were well past the dangerous pitch where the disaster had come, when we were near Wynds Point, at the great dent in the middle of the Beacon's face, the carriage halted where the unwalled, unfenced western body of the Beacon came down to the road. Here I was helped to get down, and was shown how I was to go alone on the hill,

13

just below the first great trench, and watch them coming to me by the usual path to the summit.

It was my first free walk upon any Malvern hill, and it happened to be summer, and after a rainy day. The great heave of the hill was marvellous with young fern, with tiny trickles of water and many flowers, and the magical soft slippery turf of summer, all glittering with the last rain, and noisy with bumble-bees.

Here I could scramble up in a world of shining beauty to the pitch of the lowest trench, seeing all manner of strangeness: the tiny bones of rabbits or birds, occasional eggshells of thrush, blackbird or wood-pigeon, stray feathers that I could not identify, and the scufflings and tunnellings of rabbits. From these I came at once to the barren turf of the steepness of the rampart, the abrupt slippery climb to the top of it, and then the leap or slither down into the trench, which ran round the hill, and was ever silent save for a strange noise of wind and ever somewhat terrible as though haunted.

The trench was not to be lingered in: it was too lonesome and uncanny. I got out of it at once, and kept to the top of the lowest parapet, in which someone, at some unknown time, had cut a little sloping alley-way or postern. In later years I often went there, and wondered who had used that little narrow steep entrance, and had done it so neatly, and for what?

In a few minutes I was with my party, on the usual easy path that most people use when climbing the Beacon. I climbed with them to the top,

'And lo, Creation widened in man's view'

At that time, Bredon Hill was the place that I looked for. It was pointed out to me, not very far away, a conspicuous hill in the valley below me. But I could not see its tower nor the great lump of stone, the Boundary Stone, left by some glacier of the past, as I had been told. Having looked in vain for that I asked for the Wrekin; that, too, was pointed out to me. I was also shown the Titterstone, or Tottering Stone, that weighed some tons yet was so marvellously poised that a child could rock it. Of these, the Wrekin was the most thrilling to me, for I was told that it had been a volcano, and had had a crater spouting fire, and that now the lava had become solid and had made a stopper to its crater so that it spouted no more.

After this, we walked down the hill, taking a look at some of the trenches, which gave me the feeling that they have never failed to give me, of vastness, of roughness, and of something vast, rough and uncanny with a life of its own, like itself everlasting and strange; not inhuman, but not human.

I have that sense of it still, and marvel at it. The rough wild hill is impressed with a rough wild life that is strangely greater than anything alive now.

I have no recollection of the return journey to Ledbury; possibly I was asleep before we reached home. I felt, later, that I had been in some way linked with the Herefordshire Beacon; I have that feeling still; and that somehow it is too great for the men of this time to interpret.

People there had made the earth their father and protection; and the earth remembered that, and they, as parts of the memory of the earth, could still impress and terrify. Often they have terrified me.

It is likely that I was taken to see the cave of St Waum the Hermit, and his Well, just below the cave. I have an uncertain memory of seeing both these sights, but I was tired with excitement and interest at that time and could record no more. I often saw them later.

Some places seem to have a memory and a living spirit. We do well to keep such places holy, and to seek what they have to tell us.

I know that this visit to the Herefordshire Beacon unsettled and excited me. I had now seen the Beacon, the Wrekin, Wenlock Edge, Bredon Hill, and distant May Hill, with its famous Ploughman then ploughing with his team. All these places had been held by the Ancient Britons, who must have been remarkable fellows to have held them.

We had, apparently, dispossessed the fine fellows and killed them or driven them away and taken their possessions. We were the English, of course, and they were the Ancient Britons, who were the ancestors of the surviving Britons, the Welsh.

Surely something was wrong in our estimates of ourselves and of the Welsh? Had Effan Chones really trowned the tuck and stolen the monkey?

And who had stolen Effan Chones's land, look you?

'It was too hard a knot for me to untie.'

Those were my first memories of the climbing of any Malvern hill, and of the wonderful Beacon, but I have fainter, perhaps earlier, memories, of one or two ridings up one of the hills from Malvern town on a donkey. I remember also a picnic near St Anne's Well in Malvern, a very early occasion when a sheep came for buns, and being at last denied raided the spread feast and took them.

The Malvern hills with their donkeymen stick in my memory for another thing. They showed for sale small pieces of purple crystal which, they said, could be found on the hills among the rocks. I never saw such crystals among the rocks there, and have wondered since then where they could be found.

At the time, they seemed most precious, but crystal of a crude kind could be found in any heap of stones broken for the local roads. We had eyes for crystally bits, and brought them home, hoping that they might be pronounced to be jewels, but they never were. However, we collected starry bits, and often wetted them to make them bright; and supposed, perhaps, that it made them of good water.

Sometimes when we were in Malvern for a stay, we were able to drink the water in the famous well of St Anne. At this place we felt that we could distinguish a special 'flavour of silver' just as the water reached the throat; and thought ourselves really enriched by the precious draught.

5

Bredon Flood

In that early time I went much to a part of Bredon Hill of which I have glad memories.

I know that once, while there, I was taken to a crossing of roads, with wide grassy borders in which (near the fences) one could find in season wild white violets of an unusual kind.

White violets are common near Ledbury, and unbelievably fragrant. These, in memory, were less fragrant, but for some peculiarity of soil were of a more reddish tinge; much more markedly red in the under petal than the ordinary white violet known to me, the red of these was a deeper red and covered more of the petal. We thought that they should be called red violets.

I have vivid memories of their unusual abundance and of the depth of their reddish tinge.

Long after I had forgotten about them, and the place where they grew, I came upon the spot while walking there. It was not then violet time and there were no violets on view; but that was the place, not far from Pershore, so famous once for its perry. Perhaps the quality in the soil that made the perry good gave a special grace to the local violets.

During another early visit to Bredon there was a fine flood, I suppose in the very late winter (in February-fill-dyke) for it was warm wet weather with good long daylight.

It had been very wet and

'When Bredon Hill puts on her cap
You men of the Vale, beware of that.'

The rain had fallen in abundance, and had filled the Avon valley as full as it could hold. A lot of hilly ground feeds the lower Avon in wet weather, and this flood was remembered for a good many years.

The sight of any unusual show of water has ever been a delight to me; and here to my joy, just at the brink of it was this unusual spread, a record flood of a river a hundred times the power of Leddon in a valley worthy of her might. My cup of bliss was for the moment as full as it wanted to be.

But at this moment, two young men appeared who had business in the deep waters and asked me 'would I not come with them?' In rapturous bliss I went with them down the little lane to the boat-house, and there I was at the brink of a greater flood than I had ever seen, and nearer to danger than I had ever been; but having no thought of danger with these two young men, who spoke as if they were used to boating on floods a little below Niagara Falls.

They had not exactly the keys of Paradise but they had the keys of the boat-house, and in a moment they unlocked the door and there I was in the boat, in the talking water, among the lipping relics on an expanse with no visible banks, but with drowned hedges sticking up from muddy moving water.

What occasion had called them to the flood I never knew, or have forgotten if I did know. I was with them for perhaps half an hour, so full of joy that my head could not record it. Such half-hours cannot be described; they may be sung of, perhaps, in ecstatic memory, or in dream.

I had later memories of Bredon, but this was the intensest.

Three other early memories of that visit remain: somebody there made me a great blob of marvellous sugar-candy; a man showed me a place near the church where an adder had 'sat up and sissed at him'; and a place where another man had heard a fox bark (to show me how bold a fox could be: like the adder he had been quite near the church).

6

The Hereford and Gloucester Canal

To my young mind, the most wonderful thing near my home was the canal, where barges passed all day long between Gloucester and Hereford.

I believe that this canal had been begun in the year 1797 to run from the Severn near Gloucester to Hereford (about thirty-three miles), on the line Newent–Ledbury, if the profits permitted.

In those years of war, the scheme lagged, and was much delayed. There seems to have been a halt in the work at some point (about Newent?). It seems to have reached Ledbury in the peace of 1814, and stayed there, somewhere near the present gas-works, from the time of Waterloo. Then followed a long pause before the work went further. I know nothing of its completion, but in time it pushed on to Hereford, and was then called the Hereford and Gloucester Canal.

The Great Western Railway line presently linked Hereford with Worcester.

The canal that meant so much to me was a doomed concern at the time, though I did not know it. I saw its last prosperous years.

To my young self it was the main wonder and delight in life. It crossed the fields directly below my home, and wherever it appeared it heightened Life.

It seemed to urge the young soul to adventure on, away, away, to glorious Hereford; it seemed to tell of wonders, to try to get to which would be wonderful. It, in itself, was wonderful.

In my memory, I cannot think why, all the barges are outward bound going from the south northward towards Hereford, in the two miles of flat valley offering there. I have no memory whatever of barges going towards Gloucester, except one which on the voyage south paused at Bosbury bridge to let another pass.

The canal, its barges, horses, people and wonder, made the great romance of every day and the beauty of some of its reaches I can never forget.

I suppose that 250 yards after passing the fields near my home, the canal went under the bridge over the road to Hereford, and there reached what was in effect a kind of primitive port. The tow-path was always on the western shore, but on the eastern shore at this point was a small, somewhat untidy, field, or grass patch (in wet weather much seamed with spouting springs).

This field was, to my mind, a wonderful seaport. A good many barges tied up to the bank of this field, to discharge and load cargo, to wait for cargo or to do road-repairs. Carts coming with cargo across this grass patch gave it the look of untidiness that it has in my memory.

The field was shut in to the north by the embankment of the Great Western Railway, which ran across it by bridge with the line linking Hereford with Worcester. The embankment continued from the bridge, to cross the low-lying fields in the valley of the little River Leddon further west.

This embankment on the north and the Hereford Road

on the south of this untidy patch gave the place a shut-off appearance, a seclusion, and a seeming peace. It was, anyhow, a place of rest. The horses of the waiting barges moored there very likely had stabling close at hand. The plot seemed a kind of anchorage or harbour, where the crews could take aboard what they wanted before going on to the unknown. They were at the gateway of the unknown.

This gateway was the Railway Bridge, a very terrible place, for below it was the drowning place of unwanted dogs. But when once one had passed the bridge, towards the north, the beauty of the canal began to overwhelm the soul with joy.

Beyond that bridge of drowned dogs for some quarter of a mile or more a lovely reach stretched to Heaven and the sun that shines in childhood. In memory that reach is always sunny, and at one point in it, about halfway along it, some lucky and happy boys were free to swim. The water in that reach seemed always to be clear: fish would rise and moorhens would paddle (often with their little dusky chicks), and the bank yielded the most adorable flowers.

Sometimes, in that clear reach, I was allowed to fish, with a rapture of hope that the fish might be a goldfish, or some other wonder; and though I never had a bite, never once, I had more joy of hope than most men, far more.

Then, going as I did, from the known and inhabited world to an unpeopled country, for there was then no house in those parts and perhaps no house at all was then easily visible from that tow-path, there was the feeling that all that path by all that clear water, must lead to Paradise;

and sure enough it did; in every Maytime it surely did.

To most mariners, the wonder of the sea is the land you come to. In May or June the wonders of the canal were what seemed (then) to me to be the Fortunate Islands, one on each side of the clear water near the bridge of the Bosbury Road.

There on each side of the waterway, in a shallow to the east, and on a hillock to the west, were the Fortunate Islands; not islands at all but patches of flowers unmatched for colour and enchantment, not easy to describe.

On the eastern side, where some spring had opened the canal bank to the field, a clump of the yellow flag flowers grew profusely, and with them the adorable rarity (to children) of bulrushes, that no child could safely wade to try to pick. Each plant in that watery bed was of a rarity and beauty not to be told.

On the western side, in the hillock, grew surely every flower that can gladden a child's heart with ecstasy.

On the little, strange, fertile, yet seemingly unowned, uncultivated hillock there grew, each in its season, so many flowers that win a child's heart that I will name only two, neither very common. One was Jack-go-to-bed-at-noon, that closes its flowers at midday, as I could see for myself; the other was, I suppose, a sport or escape from some forgotten crop: a clump of a strong white clover deeply tinged with pink in the blossom but remaining a white (or slightly yellowed white) not a pink blossom.

It was a noble clover unlike any other that I have ever seen. It remains in my memory as a symbol of what can be achieved, by a mingling of intense thought with human clay. I have never seen any flower of more intense beauty.

The Clover Cop
O, white (but red-tinged) thing that thrusts
From all this glory, all these lusts,
O living marvel, that atones
For all this sorrow among bones
With promise of eternal peace
When in man's heart the fires cease.

My memory tells me that there was a good deal of traffic on the canal. I must have seen many barges passing on to Hereford. The barges were small and made from about two and a half miles to three miles in the hour. Wind would have delayed them a good deal in stormy times, but delay could not have harmed their usual cargoes. The crews were either two men or a married couple. I have lively memories of the woman steering with her most becoming head-dress of a milkmaid's cap flapping on her cheeks, and the husband ahead minding the horse, and often singing, or knitting, or flinging words over his shoulder to the wife.

Sometimes these glorious people begged the little boy to come aboard, and showed me the marvellous cabin, bright as a new pin, with its bunks and gear, the most wonderful abodes on earth. I do not doubt that the crews had a hard life of it in the main, working cargo in port, and having the horse to groom, and the entire ship to keep clean, in addition to being either at the helm or minding the horse when under way. I suppose that a day's tow would bring them to Ledbury from Gloucester, and that another day's tow would bring them to Hereford. They would then have (as I suppose) to work to discharge the cargo, then to clean the hold, and take in whatever was going east. The work must have been often pretty hard, but never hard for long, and always varied in scene and company, and never exhausting.

It seemed the most perfect form of life that the world had to offer to the grown-up.

I had a belief that Ledbury was a sort of sailors' Fiddlers' Green, where all these canal people rejoiced and made merry together. I do not know what had made me think this, but I believed it. I was not often in the Bye Street, but believed that that was their Sailor Town, and that there, when lamps were lit and little boys in bed, they would meet and make merry, and tell of the dangers of the deep.

The canal, as far as I have seen it, had about one lock in every two miles of its course.

In a very severe winter, the frost might stop navigation for a time. The frozen reaches then made good skating. I sometimes met a man who had skated from Ledbury to Hereford and back, about twenty-five miles, in the course of one winter day. He said that it was an easy run, but that he had not trusted the ice under some of the bridges.

For many years, the image of some of the well-known reaches of this water came into my dreams, mingled with scenes from the river and its millstream. Often, too, the scenes of the unknown reaches, far from Ledbury, and away towards Hereford, appeared in dreams, made splendid by tropical forests, abundant cataracts, and caves of fire.

I will not call the canal a liberal education: it was more of an invitation to inquiry: an inquiry that could not then be followed, whatever wonders it offered. It was Romance to me.

7

Terrors

MORE than eighty years ago, England was mainly an agricultural land, with a small population that raised most of the food it ate.

London was big, of course, but a man starting in the City could walk out of London easily, in any direction, in the inside of one afternoon.

In the English country, the farmers permitted footpaths with stiles in many fields, even in the arable fields, and never left their cattle in such fields. If there were a footpath one could feel sure that there would be no danger.

But Hereford was a famous cattle country, supplying breeding-stock for the ranches of Australia, South America and the United States. The grasslands of Hereford bred a vast head of cattle, and it behoved anyone venturing into her pastures to make quite certain that no one had left a gate open, or failed to repair a gap in a fence. There were cattle and a bull on most farms, and it was well to make sure, if one could, that no cattle were in a field before venturing within it. Cattle are swift movers for short distances, and quick in attack.

All children in that happy land were told of the dangers of cattle, and most of them had a terror of bulls, of weaning cows, or of spirited bullocks in company. Few children could grow up without hearing of some of the results of careless trespass in the pastures. All nurses of the young knew what had happened to little boys who had disregarded the warnings of the wise, and had been gored, or tossed, or overtaken at the fence 'and they saw the bull gore him and kneel upon him, and gore him dead, so that his own mother couldn't know him'.

I cannot describe the terror that these tales wrought in me.

My friends, the farm people towards Bosbury, had shown me a smooth and silent and quiet bull in his stable. He had a ring in his nose, and I was told that with the ring in his nose he could not do any harm, if the man knew his work and watched him.

I would hear this, and be comforted; but later, when it was darker, how could one be sure?

Then, when I went to bed, what agonies of terror would come, that a bull might be under the bed, waiting till I was really asleep; and then, when I was really asleep, what agonies of terror, when . . .

Sometimes the nightmares would be appalling. Remembering the bull in his stable, so quiet, so splendid, I would dream, perhaps, that I had gone to see him, and had then (madly) gone to the spacious loft of his byre, where one could often see little mice nibbling and flitting about.

Ah, but in my dream, I would go along the upper storey of the loft, among the hay and perhaps the old bee-skeps or other stores, and watch the birds come with grubs for their little chickens . . .

and then,

ah, then,

I would hear some tiny rustle behind my back, and then there would be the bull creeping up the stairs to me, making almost no noise, and now able to see me, for his eyes would be flashing fire.

Sometimes, it would not be like that, but I would be walking in the green pastures by the river, somewhere under the piers of the viaduct, looking at the kingfishers, for there were always some there, nesting in the banks . . .

and then,

ah, then,

there would be a braying of bulls, and all the herd would come round the corner at me to have my blood.

I sometimes feel sure that I fainted with the terror of such moments.

Horned cattle were not the only terrors of that country; there were two other great terrors: the gipsies the chief, and the hornets the lesser, gipsies lasting all the year, the hornets for not more than about seven months in the year.

Gipsies I saw at various times, either on the roads or camped by the road on some more than usually wide selvage or grassy way for horsemen. Just beyond the enchanted islands at the canal to the south of the Bosbury bridge, there was a copse where gipsies sometimes camped for weeks together. I know not what they did there but they stayed there for long times together, with about a dozen horses and half a dozen vans.

Now I was well disposed to gipsies: I used to see them on market days and admired their waistcoats, their gold buttons, and their shunning of the ways of grown-ups in their choice of vans as homes and the breadth of England for their doorsteps.

But my nurses told me that I must never never listen to gipsies, because they stole little boys and sold them. They said that they would be smiling and sweet, and would tempt me away from home, just round the corner some-where, to come to see a pretty bird or to eat a little sugar-cake that they had specially for a boy like me. It would be in vain for me to say No, for they could persuade any foolish child; and O, if I went with them to see the bird or the sugar-cake, I should be lost indeed.

Once aboard the lugger, the child was lost.

The gipsies, so the women told me, at once took the child's clothes, and rubbed his body with 'walnut juice', always with walnut juice, because it made all the skin brown. Then they dressed the child in some rags of their own, 'so that his own parents would not know him', and at once would start off the van and be ten miles away before the parents missed the child.

Then they would so beat and terrify the child that he would give no trouble to them, nor bring them to justice. Then speedily they would sell him to a sea-captain, who would shortly sail him to America and sell him for a slave or apprentice.

These things were told to me as warnings of what certain wicked gipsies would do to me if they got the chance. They made me very careful to try not to give them the chance, and to beware of soft-spoken men and women in vans, with blarney and sweet cakes, for they were stealers of children, and would sell them when caught.

Those who warned me of the gipsies were warning me in good faith of a real danger that must have become very rare indeed, but had been common enough for more than two centuries. To this day, we have in the daily speech of the English the slang name for this crime. We speak of it still as 'kid napping' or child stealing, though few who use the phrase now suspect that they use thieves' slang. It was a profitable common crime in the mid-seventeenth and eighteenth centuries.

I do not doubt that in the early nineteenth century it was still sometimes possible and profitable, and that plausible people in vans moved about the English country beguiling children into their clutches, and selling them for what they might fetch. I think these plausible people would have been strangers to the countrysides where they sought their prey, but several women assured me that 'the gipsies' were the guilty people. I do not suppose that gipsies were the guilty parties, but I much feared it then, and took great care to avoid dark strangers with honey cakes lest

'Goodbye house and goodbye home
I should be for the Moors and martyrdom.'

In the seaports of my youth, in various countries, the kidnappers sought and caught their prey without much risk or difficulty. Their yearly captures must have numbered hundreds.

The third dread of my childhood was the hornet, a big handsome wasp always very common in Herefordshire, but occasional in most English counties.

I was told in infancy that three stings from a hornet would kill a man, and was left to judge for myself that one might be enough to kill a boy. I had many chances every summer of putting hornet stings to the proof.

I found that hornets were not easily stirred to anger, and that they left people alone if the people would leave them alone. I was never stung by a hornet, and have never met anyone who had been stung by one. Some writers who know more of them than I have felt as I have felt,

31

that they are peaceable when left alone. I do not doubt that the community would defend itself if attacked, and might then be terrible.

A few years ago I had a very populous hornets' nest near my home, and saw one sunny day a sight that I had never heard of, nor expected: I saw the hornets swarming; as I supposed, when a new queen left with her following. I stood near a yew-tree hedge watching the swarm of hornets, not less than forty, as I reckoned. They paid no attention to me, and I could not see the new queen; but I watched the beauty of their flight with admiration.

Many years ago I used sometimes to see the scorched ruins of a burnt willow tree near the millstream. The willow tree in its old age had contained a strong colony of hornets, which seemed likely to menace a farmer's stock coming to rub against the tree, and therefore prompted some young men to blow up the tree with blasting powder in a dark summer night.

The feat was long before my time, but it was a good deal talked of. Not much is known about hornets by country people. They believe and fear the worst of them, but they have the knowledge that some hornets of every nest are night movers, or foragers, or workers, and that in any night attack some hornets will be awake and ready to repel boarders. However, the young men, who knew that they were planning a feat of real danger, made their plans and carried them out as follows:

Those who were in the plot (I daresay four or five) had spied-out the willow tree and its apparent or probable rottennesses. They decided that the deed should be done at night; that one man, their trustiest and steadiest hand, should go boldly to the tree in the dark and lay, with a sure hand, the tin of blasting powder at the vital point, with the allotted length of fuse. This, if done calmly and without bungling, in the dark, should suffice. The muffled man should then make at once for safety, away from the other conspirators, who would linger near the millstream and at once fire the fuse.

They had a good length of well-proven fuse, which could be depended on.

I saw the hero of the evening in much later life, but never was in his confidence. He must have been a steady fellow. The night proved to be fine. The gang went to a bridge over the millstream, and the chosen spirit took the powder and the fuse. He had taken a good and near view of the tree in daylight, and had some notion of where to approach it and how to leave the powder. It was not a deep darkness, but a summer night, and some of the hornets were up and busy. It was no light adventure to him. He no doubt firmly believed that one or two hornet stings might kill him, and that three certainly would be fatal.

I think that he had ten or eleven yards to go to lay his bomb with the fuse attached. In the story, as told to a later admiring generation, he advanced quietly and calmly, well masked and covered, but showing no fear. On reaching the tree, he laid the tin as he had planned, in the spot he had noted. He was aware that the hornets were awake, but he was not attacked.

As he had decided and arranged, he did not return to the gang, but walked steadily and swiftly in another direction, well away from the gang who were now to fire the fuse. He was to meet them in another place after the explosion. He was said to have had some trepidation as he

33

retreated, not knowing how cool his friends might be, and half expecting to be involved in the explosion with old willow tree, blasting powder and dying hornets.

The explosion was delayed. He was able to cross the field to its gate, and wait there.

But now, as no explosion followed, he was sure that something had gone wrong.

What had delayed them?

He felt that they had dropped the matches into the water, or wetted the fuse, or were failing to strike a light in the breeze that was blowing. The question for him was, should he go back to help them if they were in trouble? But they might not be in trouble. They might be only giving him plenty of time to get out of range. If he went now, he might arrive at the tree just as the fireworks began.

Or had the farmer caught them there and put a stopper on any fireworks? He waited for a minute or two, being unable to see his mates, and wondering what had happened. Something had gone wrong. It had been decided that there should be no calling or speaking while they were present, lest they should attract other people to the place.

He was at the point of going back to them, when he saw the flame of the fuse, something like a slow moving snake on the ground. There was no doubt that the fuse was alight and on its way to the charge. He saw the little fire near the tree; and then, O then . . .

'There came a burst of thunder sound,' and the rotten old willow went up in glory: it was said to have burned till morning; and the hornets died with their young.

The delay had been caused by a little puddle near the

tree. The gang had had to fit some feet of new fuse and relight it.

The jagged ruin of the tree stood in a charred condition for many years.

8

The Flooded Valley with its Moles

THE low-lying fields crossed by the railway viaduct were watercourses subject to flood. The little river and its mill-stream made a sad mess of that valley in wet weather, and of every boy who ventured near them to sail a toy boat or boats.

The appearance of one of the water-meadows in that valley after some days of rain was remarkable. The fields were flattish, with a general slight slope to take the waters south-eastward. The rain, shall we say, was not excessive, but freshening. It gave the clay of the valley a brighter red, and the multitudes of moles made each field pocky with the scarlet pimples of the molehills. The moles must have been in great numbers, living as they did on earthworms in multitude. But I feel that one tends to over-estimate their numbers. Moles are said to be always hungry, and in floodtime, which was their gorging time, the surface clay in which they burrow is fairly easy to them. I have been impressed by their speed in burrowing. One could stand in any part of such a field, and be amazed at the sight of so many hundreds of molehills. Standing still, watching, one could see here and there the trembling in a mole-run where the mole moved after his prey. One specially big field of the sort was like a great body red with a raging measles. One could have counted the blotches of the molehills by hundreds at such a time. The mortality among the earthworms must have been great; but one never found that the moles suffered. Some instinct saved them from staying too long in the toothsome lowlands, and they left for higher ground (one supposed) before the water could drown them.

Their enemy in those days was the mole-catcher, a countryman who made a living by clearing or thinning the mole population in those fields. The mole-catchers were a race apart, so I was told; they did not engage in the usual labours of the farm, but covenanted to clear such and such fields, and then proceeded, by trap, to clear the area.

The mole was said to be easily killed by strangulation (most creatures are). Against the multitude of moles there came the professional mole-catcher who in every district made war upon them.

Most of the mole-catchers then in the district set hazel springes with string nooses, that the mole in passing released. The hazel wand sprang up and the cunning noose choked and slew the mole that had released it. The springes were set with much skill and were very deadly.

The steel nipping-trap was just beginning to take the place of the springe, but there would be few of these in any field in the early 'eighties.

The mole-catcher that I used to see always wore wonderful waistcoats of moleskins. It was the dream of most boys to grow up and to wear a moleskin waistcoat made from the moles slain by one's own springes. Such waistcoats were remarkable and noticeable, they conferred distinction, for not many had them, and each needed a dozen or twenty skins, for they were 'cut high and stretched low' and had to cover winter underwear.

I saw one mole-catcher wearing a waistcoat of mole-skin that was said to be buttoned by real, golden guineas.

I think that some young men who lived in the country and cared for the sports that were favoured there pur-chased moleskins from the catchers and had them made up by tailors.

Perhaps some of these may have caused sporting buttons to be provided for them.

It is many years since I saw a moleskin waistcoat. Perhaps the curious may still see them here and there with other relics of vanished England: the smock-frock, the corduroy trowsers tied beneath the knees, and the milkmaid's linen bonnet that was so becoming and looked so well wherever it appeared, whether in the busy market, the farmyard, or at the tiller of a barge.

9

The Hunt

A SHORT half mile from my home on the east side of the
road to Bosbury, and well back from that road, so that they
could not be seen from the road, were the kennels of the
Ledbury Hounds. The houses and stables of some of the
staff of the Hunt lay near the kennels, a little further north.

I saw the hounds at exercise very frequently and would
sometimes see them, or some of their followers, in or
near the coverts on that side of their country. They
figured largely in my interests and admirations, but not
so largely as the canal and the life of the canal.

In the hunting season I often saw them setting forth to
or coming back from a hunt. Sometimes a rider would be
with them coming home, with a fox's mask as his trophy
strapped to his saddle. Once when I was very young, I
was amazed and delighted to find the hunt, hounds,
huntsmen and riders all thrusting into our field and
checked at the garden fence, and seeking leave to come
through after their fox.

This was an unexpected wonder, but there the hounds
and hunt servants were, at check at the fence, with fifty
or sixty riders streaming up the field to them. The hounds
had been called off just in time, or they would have been
all over the garden and out on the other side. There they
were, not too well-pleased at being stopped, and there

were the Huntsman and the Master asking leave to come through to the road; and the crowd of riders increasing under my eyes.

They had come on a hot scent down the westerly wind, and there they all were; the hounds vexed, and perhaps earning a rate or two, and some little delay in the coming of the permission to come through: a minute perhaps (which I enjoyed if the hounds didn't). Then, at a word the gates opened, and the Huntsman gave the word, trailing his whiplash and with the word from him the hounds were at his horse's heels, and every possible care was given to the garden by those who took its two ways to the road. Hounds and followers were on the road in a couple of minutes, but they could not make anything of their fox there. Something had killed the scent in the few minutes of the check, perhaps cattle on the road, or other traffic. They had to lift hounds and try some of the great coverts of the Frith.

The wonder of the sight, the eager hounds fresh and excited by the half mile of their hunt (for they had found at Wall Hills), and the joy of seeing all the hunt so near at hand, and so near a fox who yet was then out of danger, stirred me to paint a picture of the scene, over which I took great pains, and much red paint.

Early in every year the kennels made use of a field near the railway station as the birthplace and breeding-quarters of the pack. The place was given over to little kennels, each with privacy and a special run, and con-spicuous notices to the public:

'Beware of the Hound Bitches
Very Dangerous.'

10

The Outcast

THE great rookery only two fields away greatly interested me. I was told that if I found a broken rook's egg in January in any year, I should have a happy year. But luck was out, seemingly: I never did.

One afternoon, there was a great disturbance in the rookery, for no apparent reason. A knowledgeable woman told me that they were having a law-suit with one of their members, and that I should know what they decided presently.

I do not know how she knew, but she must have been wise in the ways of those wise birds, for the next morning she was proven right. She said, 'Come down to the pond. You will see for yourself. They have found one of the rooks guilty and turned him out of the rookery.'

I followed her down to the pond. I saw that the rookery had ceased to trouble itself with the wicked one. Soon I saw the wicked one himself. He was sitting in a sapling at the edge of the pond, looking very sick indeed.

His feathers were (as it seemed) faded, dirty and staring. His look was that of one sick and without hope.

He did not heed our presence near him: he had been cast out by his community, and our community was a poor thing in comparison with his. We were a poor wing-less set who could not lift into the air nor poise on an upper branch fifty or eighty feet in blowing wind. He made no attempt to avoid us. He had been cast out of his community, and that was the end for him.

He did not seem defiant at all: he seemed to feel his situation acutely and to ask for death.

The woman who brought me to see him said that he had committed some crime against rook law, that he was judged for having done this thing, this sin, against rook law. I was not quite sure about this myself. To me he looked very ill indeed and possibly a danger to his community. None of his community had had any mercy for him, and to me he seemed to need mercy, and I would have asked for mercy for him had I known to whom to appeal, and how. He died during the day, and was given a more or less Christian burial under the yew trees.

II

The Angel

SOMEWHERE in my very early time I saw something that still puzzles me; it was a strange experience. It happened in a mild but wild morning of blowing, clearing weather, with the wind at about west, or west by north, with much clearing cloud going by. I was out of doors with a friend when I saw a strange cloud-formation of rough and wild aspect coming eastward a little to the south of me, taking an easterly course, much lower down than most clouds, and coming fast in that blowy day.

The cloud was a big cumulus cloud in the shape of two vast human bodies arm-in-arm, intent upon their journey. They had only two legs between them, and these two legs trailed below their bodies and seemed to bend, as they dangled, from the pace of their going.

When I saw them, the thing was near at hand, and I could not have seen them for more than a few seconds of intense interest. It never occurred to me that the thing was a low cumulus cloud in an unusual day. It seemed to me that the thing was alive with a kind of life of its own, and that it was blissfully bent on the enjoyment of that life and rapt with the joy of it, the two figures as one.

It rushed upon its way and was utterly out of sight from where we were in a very few startled seconds. Trees

43

and other obstacles, such as the slope of a wooded hill, utterly hid it from us, but it left us both amazed.

My companion said at once that it was an angel, but I did not think so: it was too big I thought and too double. Long afterwards, I heard a man quote an old eastern proverb, that 'no angel is given two messages', and this angel had quite certainly two heads and two bodies; and though I never doubted that it was a righteous and helpful creature I was sure that it could not be an angel. It was intent with purpose: it was steering a definite course with a task to do and a purpose to fulfil. How it could have cleared the high ground to which it was heading I could not imagine, but it was intent upon its task and seemed to have enormous power.

I have seen nothing very like it since then, and rank it as one of the strangest things I have seen. I suppose it to have been a freak formation of clearing weather, and am glad to have seen it.

Neither my companion nor I had any fear of it. We both knew, somehow, that it was a benign thing. From the course it held, I have supposed that it was making for Wynds Point and Bredon Hill, bearing somebody unusual good, a message unusually happy.

12

Ermentrude

No⊤ long ago, I saw, for the first time, the neat, clear handwriting of a man whose little dog I much admired. I often saw the man, with or without his little dog, but he was not a familiar friend like the dog. He had a sister, whom I frequently saw, and liked very much; not only for her qualities, but for her possession of a work of art, beyond which human power could scarcely go, yet which she had made with her own hands.

This work of art was a pen-wiper. It showed a black velvet mouse, with beady eyes, lying on a circular mat of leaves of cloth, which wiped the pen. The mouse was the glory of the work. Art could hardly go further than that mouse. Often I was welcomed there to look at the mouse, to stroke it and admire its life-like eyes and the miraculous likeness to a mouse. Once, I remember, the maker and owner of this treasure asked me to come with her up the brook to see old Mrs ———, who lived there. I was always ready to go up or into a brook if it were not too dangerous, so I went, not knowing what was to come.

I had never been beyond a certain point in that garden and if I met old Mrs ——— I have forgotten all about her, but I know that I was taken into the garden of Paradise, where eternal beauty of water made an earthly heaven. I had a child's love for the beauty and the miracle of water which was a joy freely given in that land of springs. I had a passion for any running spring, and had the joy of seeing at least two every day of my life, though one of these was only a leaky tap.

But here my guide led me into a grassy plot where a rapturous clear spring trembled up from a hollow, with little dancing crumbs of pleasure in its depth and the sunlight in its going. It fulfilled (to me) my sense of what a stream should be; a revelation of purity and beauty and an image of abundance, it ought to be brim full. This spring had fullness. It was

'without o'er-flowing full,'

it was full to the very brim of its little meadow channel, where the tops of the grasses caught some of the passing bubbles.

I know nothing more of that water nor what became of it; I never was very near to it since that one visit. But I did certainly see that marvellous spring at its gushing source at the foot of the eastern hill, one of seven such, once known to me as the most perfect of the seven, having the channel full to the brim, and swaying the tops of the grasses in its meadow.

My friend, the lady who owned the mouse, married soon after this. I was taken specially to see the happy couple leave the Church and mount into an open carriage drawn by four horses, with two marvellous postillions in red. I think still of her grace, and am glad that she saw me and smiled to me.

I never saw her again; and never wrote to her in after years to thank her for these memories of her; but seeing her brother's writing has brought her vividly to memory. Mice meant much to me as a child, multitudes of little mice behaving like men; and abundant beautiful running waters have meant much to me at all times.

She was most kind to a little child, and took me into that enchanted garden, and smiled to me on that day of her wedding.

13

Closing the Canal

AT some time early in my life the managers of the canal and of the railway decided that the canal should cease, and that its course from near Gloucester to Ledbury should be taken by a branch railway line.

The canal from Ledbury to Hereford was to be allowed to lapse, and become in time agricultural land again. The existing railway from Worcester to Hereford would easily take its place, with a little improvement, with changes and the making of switches.

At Ledbury station, and close to it to the west, there were some important changes, most of which were of great interest to me. We could hardly take any of our familiar walks without seeing these.

The new line from the old canal had to make a great sweep from the course of the canal to the approach of the station. This was to be carried on a new embankment. The embankment entailed a new bridge over the Hereford Road, and this, and matters of structure in Ledbury station, entailed much quarrying and cutting of stone somewhere in the unknown world to the east of the station.

We knew nothing of it, but there came days when the very last barge went past to Hereford, and unnoticed and unmourned the last barges from Hereford slipped past us back to Gloucester, and the last engineers ceased to

48

ensure water in the miles of the waterway. Most of the canal between Ledbury and Gloucester ceased or was filled-in.

The canal to the north of us held a good deal of water in places, for some years to come.

Almost at once a pinkish stone was brought to the Hereford Road, and workers were there cutting, shaping it and laying it in the lower courses of what was to be a bridge. We picked up tiny scraps of the stone for our collections, and wondered if its sparkling fragments could be gold dust or jewel.

Soon, the curving bridge was built, and the embankment was pushing beyond it towards us with wonderful speed. On the embankment top we could see two engines of ancient type, one of which was called Puffing Billy, and the other some more stately name. The earthwork was manned by gangs of Public Works men who soon could be seen high up on the embankment top with trucks and horses working all day long at a game delightful to us to watch. They were employed in building the embankment by trolley loads of earth.

The loaded trolleys were drawn along the top of the work by clever horses who knew exactly, or were made exactly to stop and turn aside at the proper instant. The horse went aside, but the truck went on and at the critical moment at the right spot was checked and tipped with its tons of material. We could never see the device at work, but they delighted by their precision and skill. The embankment was soon a wall to shut us from the sight of the old canal bed. There was now no walking along that arm of its old course, but we could still use the towing path leading towards Bosbury.

For years, after the railway to Gloucester had been opened, men sometimes mourned for the old canal and the destruction of its fisheries. I cannot suppose that the fish in it were ever very pleasant as food, but the fishing was missed.

'It is the effort, not the deed, we prize.' There had been beautiful miles in which they could sit on Sundays, glad of a minnow or a roach, and enjoying the beauty of the scene.

In the laying of the line near Gloucester, men laid bare the bones of Welsh men killed in the Royalist cause in an attack on the Parliament's outpost there. Piety put up a monument to them on the spot where they had died with their Herefordshire comrades.

The cutting of the canal in 1797 to 1825 had lowered the great cost of coal for an average lifetime.

Now, after a rather longer lifetime, the railway Ledbury to Gloucester has been closed. What's to come is still unsure. I notice that in today's paper a man suggests a first-rate air-service.

Now and then to this day, I wonder where the Public Works men found all the earth that they tipped to make that strong embankment, shall we say half a mile long, thirty feet high, at least twenty feet broad at the top and three times that breadth at the base.

We never could see them loading the trucks, and never could find any big gap in any known landscape. No one was able to inform us. The earth was found I know not where, and used with great skill, leaving no great pit to show whence it had come.

14

The Soldiers

SOMETIMES, perhaps twice in a year, perhaps at rarer intervals, there came a memorable visitation. Word would come that the soldiers were coming, and the world changed indeed. All hands throughout the countryside prepared to receive cavalry, and life was indeed Life to everybody. I do not know what caused the visit, but from time to time some batteries of field artillery went through parts of the country, either as exercise of some sort or to encourage likely lads to enlist, or both. Some news of their coming preceded them, and I know that when they came they entered the town from the north, by the road from Hereford.

I do not know what regiments they were, but two or three batteries, of somewhat different uniforms, visited the town thus in the later summers. They made a wonderful show of skilled precision. They clattered by to the wonder and delight of all hands, some riding, others sitting on the perches provided; and difficult perches these seemed to the wondering and envious male. They went through into the town, and there parked their guns and billeted for the night, to the intensest joy of all who saw. We did not know of any enemy, but we were all cheered by their coming and slept the sounder for their presence.

Once as I watched, the column halted at our gate, waiting for an order to proceed. I saw the messenger ride up with the order, and heard the order given. Then, instantly, the marvellous machine was clattering on, seeking soldiers' fortune, and firing every heart with the longing to be with them, astride one of the chargers or perched somehow on one of the snug little seats with the guns and ammunition.

Later in my life when I was sent to church on Sunday mornings, I saw, once in each year, a church service with the local company of volunteers. Perhaps they were more than a full company, for they had a pretty full military band, and turned out for the occasion at full strength, and entered the church at the west door, up the steps, singing 'Onward, Christian Soldiers'. This was ever a noble sight, and gave a great beauty to the aisle and to memory.

It was at one of these church parades that I first understood the power of a great service on the human heart.

At the very end of these years of childhood, I saw a pitched battle fought between an army of red uniforms and an army in some less conspicuous uniform, not yet khaki, but in a dim dark shade of blue that no child would have called a colour at all.

The battle was fought from a rising ground in Eastnor Park, to defend the line of the local brook from the blue army advancing from the Malvern hills by way of Monument Hill. They fired a great deal at first, but the issue had been arranged without any hand-to-hand encounter. The blue army walked up to the red position and had tea.

15

Cut Throat Lane, etc.

ABOUT three hundred yards from my home, one came to the site of an old quarry, much overgrown with scrub. I was told that it was a dangerous place, and that a drunken man had fallen down the rock face there, and had broken his leg while trying to find his way home on a dark night. The fall had been considerable and I often marvelled that he had not broken his neck and other bones, but people told me that that would have killed him, and that the broken leg had been a mercy vouchsafed to him as a warning.

A little way past this warning rock one came to a dark forbidding gully called Cut Throat Lane, but why it was so named none could remember (or would tell a child). It seemed designed by nature for any felony, but I have never learned why it should have such a name. No one whom I have asked has been able to tell me why it was so called. I have sometimes wondered whether some men escaping from Ledbury battle in the Civil War were overtaken and killed there. When I last saw it, the place looked still as unsocial as ever. When I was some years older than the little child me who first looked upon it, I found the crumbling stone on the eastern hedge of it rich in tiny fossils then welcome to me. These are now less noticeable in that rough stone. I have seen some of its fossils in a

London museum, and coming upon them by surprise there I have felt cheered, as I have been cheered at other Hereford relics or reminders seen far from home.

An old pamphlet has led me to believe that at, in, or near this lane there was at one time a gallows on which people were hanged. This seems to me to be unlikely, for it is a secluded nook and the gallows was usually much more public, for the sake of its useful warning to the young. I do not think that men would have been gibbeted there, as the place cannot ever have been much frequented and the useful example would have been lost there. Possibly the old pamphlet preserved the fact that a man was hanged on the scene of his crime or supposed crime. It has always looked as likely to suggest a felony to anyone in a gloomy mood, being shut from the sun by woods and slopes.

Near this horrid hollow is a cheerful little hill called Kill Bury Camp, which I was told was the scene of a battle in old times, and the burial place of those killed in it. It is a pleasing little mound, and perhaps wrongfully called a camp, for it was never fortified, being too small. Probably it was originally called a tump by those who dispossessed those who called it a Kil or a Bre in times long since past and forgotten. To a child, the name, Kill Bury, seemed a good name for a camp after the victory, but I loved the place for other reasons. The little round top of the little round tump was the site of a cottage, the home of beloved friends. It was a steep little hill with steps cut or worn in the steepness rather like the ratlines in rigging. In the delightful garden at the top of the hill there were some gallinas, that cried 'Come back, come back' with delightful manners to every parting guest.

Down below the railway led into the tunnel, and near by one could see a gloomy ventilator that smoked when a train had lately passed. When in sight of this attraction, I was told of the frightful results of trespassing into a tunnel, when a train came into the tunnel after naughty boys, and the driver could not possibly see the truants until it was too late. I was told that the only thing to do, in such a situation, was to lie down between the rails and let the train pass over me: then, perhaps, 'if there were no loose chains and things' I might survive: it would all depend.

It was made pretty clear that I should not survive, whatever happened. I grew up with a horror of tunnels, and of trains charging into the tunnels with warning whistles to warn the trespassers. One who once lived above that tunnel wore for many years a big iron hook where his hand had once been, so that I could look at him and know what came to naughty boys.

16

Hopping

WILD hops are common in the hedges of Hereford. They grew very freely in the hedge that fenced the field that led to the kennels of the Hunt, near the railway bridge.

But cultivated hops grew in many farms; the county was famous for its hops and in September hop-picking became general all over the county and brought large numbers of strangers from distant cities, many who came because they loved the country, and a holiday that paid the holiday-maker, and (on many farms) gave him shelter while the picking lasted. But it also brought many from some dreadful towns, who were less welcome, and made the countryside unsafe for any unguarded woman; and certain death for any unguarded hen.

There were hop-yards close to the north and the west of Ledbury, and we, who knew the farms and farmers, always went hopping in the season. The pickers always welcomed us, for we did certainly pick a lot of hops with them, and helped to earn them their due as pickers. We enjoyed the work, for it was not work to us, nothing but an hour's afternoon amusement. Had it been work to us, as to the pickers bent above the crib all day picking in the sun, we might have changed our tune.

The pickers were always kind and welcoming to us and

we enjoyed it all, save one thing – that the pickers insisted on: we had to be put into the crib.

There were many cribs in each hop-yard. The crib or cratch, an open trough, I suppose about nine or ten feet long and two feet across, is a kind of elongated manger made of canvas secured to a wooden frame; it stands about as high as an ordinary table. The hop-vines are brought across the crib and the pickers pick the hops from the vines into the crib. Two sailors' hammocks, put end to end, without their clews, would make a good crib.

It was the law of the hop-yard that every picker must be put into the crib before he could be allowed to pick. This was the old custom of the yards, and was always exacted. Such customs exist in many kinds of harvest from very ancient times, to mark a propitiation or a thanksgiving, and if this had been explained to every novice asking to be allowed to pick all would have been well.

Like other children, I loved picking hops, and looked forward to it, thinking, perhaps, that I was really working and helping the pickers. (I daresay that my total labours in this way may have earned a few souls some fraction of a sixpence.)

But like many other little children I was scared of being taken by rough strangers and plunged into the crib, by some man or woman who called it a cratch, and then rolled in the rather sticky canvas in the fragments of hops. This was the price that one had to pay, and it was never cruelly done.

Later, one could pick and pick till it was time to go. Then, with both hands dark and very sticky (and tasting bitter when licked) one could shake hands with one's hosts at the cratch and wish them a happy holiday.

17

The Roman Road

I MAY have been born within a mile of a Roman road or within a mile of a Roman camp, or a settlement of Romanized Britons. There is some dispute as to which. I have been on the site of the so-called camp several times in blackberry seasons, and have seen something resembling an earth wall or rampart there. I have also been along parts of the Roman road.

When I first went to it, I was being taken to tea somewhere near it on a very wet afternoon. As we neared the Roman road, we came to a grassy space near the road where a big gathering of gipsies had pitched their camp. They had several wagons and more horses than usual. As we drove slowly through this settlement, we passed a small fire, where an old woman sat under a sack. She was smoking a short cutty-clay pipe and had a face of extraordinary good nature.

I had never before seen a woman smoking, and should have remembered her for this, but she smiled and waved to us in the most friendly way, and I knew at once that she would never kidnap me and sell me to the foreigner after staining me with walnut juice. She was thanking us for going slowly through the camp and not splashing people or scaring the horses.

The Roman road beyond this was still a road, but I

remained more interested in her, and hoped that she was not getting wet through.

Long afterwards I drove that road again with a man who told me that near that place was a county boundary, a great place for prize fights in the old days of fighting on grass in the open air.

'They pitched the ring on one side of the county boundary,' my friend said, 'and if the county magistrates interfered they moved across into the other county. They could generally finish before the other magistrates got going.'

18

The Stag

In the park at Eastnor, in a well-fenced and beautiful seclusion, there were many deer.

I had seen them now and then at a distance, moving in slow state among the wildness of the southern Malverns. I was to see one for a moment in a field near my home.

I do not know what had led to the event, but it happened that one of the stags among these deer became dangerous and escaped from the park enclosure. Whether he had gored people I do not know. Local gossip, improving the story, said that he was mad and very dangerous.

Anyhow, his case had been heard, and as he was roving the world and, perhaps, impossible to catch and doctor, and certainly dangerous to citizens, he was condemned.

I was indoors one fine morning when I heard the noise of guns and cries down in the further field. I ran to the window, and in that instant of time I heard another two shots and then a third. Then I was looking to the fields, which sloped somewhat downhill from me, and to the fences to the right which rather obscured the view there.

There was a stile over the fence at that point, and a clear view of fence, stile, and a few yards of the lower field, and as I reached the window to look out I saw a sight that I can never forget.

As I looked in that instant of time to that place of

destiny, I saw the stag leap the stile with unspeakable, matchless grace, and bound on, among shots, till hedge and the rise of the land hid him from me.

After him came the guns and men crying, and immediately I saw them lift the body of the stag that had fallen just out of sight from me.

I saw the men busy, and the dead body raised among them, and I thought my young heart would have broken, that that exquisite thing that had made that leap was now dead.

19

Circuses

PERHAPS there were more circuses then, much smaller than those of today, almost family affairs hard put to it sometimes to make a living, but never failing to bring joy, and having, all of them, much talent, of the true circus kinds and not bringing matters foreign to the true circus, such as performing seals, or monkeys riding on dogs.

One or two of the circuses of my childhood had an elephant among their performing animals. This was then a novelty, a great rarity, and welcome, for there was then in the zoo in London an elephant of fame, much in every child's imagination.

This was the popular Jumbo, the best-loved beast in the land. No child could look upon any elephant without thinking that probably the beast that he saw may have known Jumbo in the jungle, nay, might even be Jumbo's brother or uncle, or son. In any case, he was then a rarity, and a novelty in any circus and shown as a novelty not easy to provide always with sufficient fitting food.

Can I have written thus far about childhood without mention of the travelling circuses? There must have been more circuses on the summer roads then than now. They always pitched their tent in a field at the other end of the town, but always in fine weather they paraded through the town in the morning before giving a performance. The parades came as far along the road to our gate, halted briefly and turned near it, so that we saw it all in all its glory: the matchless piebalds, the floats of wonder, the unearthly beauty of the men and women, who were Red Indian Chiefs, perhaps, or Joan of Arc, or a Queen of somewhere, as matchless for beauty as for skill. All these wonders were there in full dress, promising to be more marvellous when they appeared in costume later to do their acts.

The sight of these people, with their horses and costumes, filled the entire morning with rapture and the memory with splendour and expectation. In the afternoon, as we knew, we should see these marvellous people in action. Here we only saw them pretending.

The true circus of my childhood was based on the talents of a few men and women and a few spotted or piebald horses. They performed with music, they were welcomed wherever they went in England, and travelled all over the land between May and September in a life that must have been hard, or indeed very hard. To the child the life of the company was the clown, an athlete, often a singer, a low comedian, an acrobat and a winner of every heart in the tent. His was the genius that was remembered, and though his genius seemed to some to lose its wonder in the course of time, it wore well, it could be repeated, even for a generation, and be still a delight to all who heard it. Stirred up by the ringmaster the clown would sing admirable songs that one could not forget, nor wish to forget. He uttered nothing base; all his songs were innocent, and of good report, or just merry nonsense. I have heard a clown sing songs and known them to be received as new delights that I had heard other clowns sing in other tents more than fifty years before. The clown's songs and his comic business do not grow old.

It should be remembered that the clown performs in a ring, in a tent, and has to be heard by an audience nearly all round him. He is conspicuous and important through most of the performance. What child has ever left a circus performance without longing to be allowed to become a clown and learn how to delight all sorts and conditions of men?

A never-failing delight in those circuses of eighty years ago was a turn that made children feel that it was possible to learn some of the arts needed in the business: they could be learned in the circus, being taught in the circus.

One of the popular turns showed this to all-comers in a diversion that I have not seen of late years, and have much missed. It was interesting in itself, pleased the audience, some of whom took part in it, and may possibly have been a means of helping beginners to avoid falls when learning some of the feats expected from them. The main pole or support of the big tent's body bore a light revolving derrick, that circled easily round the pole. The derrick's upper end bore a rope dangling downwards much as an angler's rod bears his line. This line at its lower end bore gear that could be buckled to a man's body.

During a performance, the ringmaster would ask for volunteers to try one of the methods by which lads were trained for some of their feats. A steady horse was in the ring saddled as for one who would ride the ring leaping through hoops at intervals. A volunteer would come into the ring, blushing but brave; he would be strapped securely to the gear, hoisted to the saddle, and the horse would start from under him, and begin a slow trot to music round the ring. In an instant the performer would be dangling in the air, and the revolving derrick would revolve so that the beginner's feet would sometimes reach the horse's saddle and would again lose it, while the audience laughed or shouted applause to the Roman who was, as it were, being butchered for their holiday.

He deserved the applause, for he had very few instants of certainty on the saddle. I think, too, that 'the garters', or leaping through the great hoop covered with tissue paper, is less performed than it was. And few ladies now leap from horse to horse as they go at speed three or four horses in a team.

Circuses now are much bigger than they were of old; there are fewer of them, and life must be easier. In the old days, the little circus must have made many 'one-night stands', coming to a little town at daybreak after a night on the road, then putting up the tent, grooming the horses, and dressing for the procession; then taking part in the procession, then returning to prepare for the afternoon show; then, after a couple of hours, the evening performance; then the packing-up of the big tent and getting off upon the road, snatching what rest could be had in the intervals of driving, tending the families or the horses, adjusting the quarrels, mending costumes, or discussing changes; taking what sleep could be had in whatever weather was going, and at all times belonging to a society that depended on itself, and was very good of its kind, and a blessing to its time.

20

Captain Jones

I HAVE an unaccountable memory of this person.

I was on a sea-wall which had steps leading to the water, and about fifty yards away was an anchored sailing vessel, probably a brigantine.

Where this was, I do not know, but I know that suddenly somewhere there was a cry that Captain Jones had fallen overboard; and looking towards the brigantine (if she were a brigantine) there was Captain Jones in the water swimming to the gangway and climbing aboard. For one in all his clothes I thought that he swam with grace and power.

I have wished that I could say that his vessel was a brig, but I don't think she was, nor do I think she was a topsail schooner.

This is all that I now know of Captain Jones.

21

The Old Mail-Coaches

THIS closing of the canal from Gloucester, and the laying of a railway in its stead, ended a line of mail-coaches that had once kept the roads there daily, to my great delight.

I did not often see them, but their passing was a wonderful sight, and left vivid memory.

In the last years of the service, a western journey was made in the afternoon at about five o'clock.

The road runs over a good level line of country. I have been told that it was taken by the coaches in one stage.

This western stage I sometimes saw.

If one went upon that road towards the time of the coach's arrival, one saw an unusual stir near the roads: people were coming to the road by every lane or field-path, for the coach carried the mails, and the Gloucester and London papers. The guards had sorted these, and had them ready to fling to the trusty messengers who would be there to collect them. Presently away in the distance there would come the note of the guard's horn, his 'yard of tin', or key-bugle. Then one would hear welcoming shouts, and then the beat, the measured unvarying beat, which is in my mind as 'the tantivy trot' of the four-in-hand drawing nearer.

As it swept past the waiting messengers and the guard flung the mail-packets to the watchers, there would be a shout, a cheer, a swift greeting, then the coach would be past, and the guard would give a note of the horn and the moment of the day would be past.

It was a great moment. There was something most noble in that balanced slither that was not a slither, but an exquisite controlled motion. The perfection of the team, the driving, the build and colour of the coach, a triumphant work of art in itself; the exhilaration of the horn, and the certainty of the delivery of the packets, all these things were the wonder of man, and each a credit to us.

Only a few days ago I saw a revived coach and four on an English road in the old inimitable slither. I was able to see again how wonderful an achievement the English made of the old coach and four, even if not 'coming down with victory' in De Quincey's phrase, but only delivering the post.

I was told that the mail-coaches had for years been despised and mocked for their slowness, in sorting, carrying and delivering the English mails.

That may have been so when the mail-service itself was a new experiment of man, but it was not so when it had reached the fine perfection that I was privileged to see.

I never saw a coach 'coming down with victory', but I often talked with one who had seen a Shropshire coach come down with the news of Waterloo, and the ending of Boney.

As the coach dashed in with the horn of triumph,

the ringers ran for the church belfry, and the world was made aware, by the prompt 'firing' of the bells, that peace had come at last.

The English do not take their pleasures sadly; they are fundamentally a deeply religious race, and are never backward in giving thanks.

22

The Forge

GOING about the country, one finds few forges nowadays. Perhaps few children now ever see a forge, with a horse being shod, 'four all round', nor hear the smith making light of his calling:

'Ah, yes, now and then, we get some rare bats.'

Generally, that is true, I think; they get the rare bats from a young horse or the more dreaded young donkey, but usually the beast being shod is patient as the sheep being shorn; and the sight of such patience, the dumb animal's trust in man, is impressive.

To me, as a child, a visit to the forge was always impressive; it was a treat connected with a visit to the canal-lock, on Ledbury's southern fringe.

There we could see the marvel of the loaded barge entering the lock at the low level. Then the gates would close; the water would be let in, with most gruesome eddyings and foamings, and in a few minutes the barge would be in the upper canal, re-horsed and away. After that, we still could call at the forge and watch a horse being shod.

If the luck were in, as it often was, there would be a giant shire-horse just brought in for treatment. We could stand at the half-door of the forge, or come right into the forge, and watch the wonderful sight of man's triple mastery over horse, metal and fire, each mastery helping his life on earth unspeakably, and all of the three then utterly beyond us.

There we would watch the fearless smith take a terrible leg in hand with a kindly grip and at once peel away the hoof, as though it were the peel of an onion. Then we would see the hot iron redden under the bellows, and smell the entrancing smell of the burnt hoof, and gasp at the skill and coolness of the smith, who fitted the shoe and nailed it sure for the roads.

23

Imagination

I AM told that I learned to read at an early age, and that I enjoyed reading more than most children.

I do not know if this were so, but I know that I found that I could tell myself stories at a very early age.

I was in the garden one day, standing near a clump of honeysuckle and looking north. As I looked, I became aware, for the first time, that I had an imagination, and that I could tell this faculty to imagine all manner of strange things, and at once the strange things, especially fantastic things, would be there in multitude to do my bidding. If I told them to put on armour and conquer France, or save Joan of Arc from being burned or Mary Queen of Scots from Fotheringay, the thing would be done, and if I disliked the doing, I had but to suggest a better method, and at once the figures for the new scene were there, perfect in form and costume, armed and horsed and with colours flying.

The faculty was extraordinary to me, and of such inner delight that I could not mention it to anyone.

I had some small foresight in the matter, and was presently to wish that I had had more.

24

Wild Flowers and Other Wild Things

The Chicory

Here, in the cuckoo's silence, we perceive
The unutterable worth of humble things,
The untaught, guideless creatures that achieve
Beauty past poetry, or pomp of kings,
The blending of all power,
All eloquence that monishes or sings,
All truth too wonderful not to believe
In this blue voiceless music of a flower.

WILD snowdrops were said to grow along the fence in a field. I used to look for them in snowdrop time, but never found them, only got happily muddy in the ditch.

In a field on the other side of the fence I found a small blue flower, that some people thought, and said, was very rare. I never heard what they found it to be; and fear that if it were really a rarity I had made it much rarer. I have now long forgotten what it looked like and what they thought it might be. I call it (now) just Sinner's Rue, or What Sinners Get.

There were strange wild things that interested me more than little blue flowers; and some of these strange things could be found in those great high pastures (if the bulls were not loose).

It was at the top of one of those great bare hill-pastures that I first saw Fairy's Rings, three or four in a line, each of great size and making a fair circle, all brown where the fairy shoes had bewitched the grass.

I never met an English person who had seen fairies, nor did I then know anyone who much believed in fairies: but there I saw their rings where many fairies had danced the moon down: and O to have seen them, up there on the hilltop, the little men with their queen.

Near there, I was told, one could see Purple Emperors, one wing of which was the purplest thing in nature. Later, I looked for such things there, yet never found.

But I did come upon a rare sight there that I have never seen elsewhere. I saw a gang of charcoal-burners.

Going up there once, we found the hilltop busy with people. They had made a vast shallow pit which was now burning or smouldering under its turf cover. The people told us that they were charcoal-burners, who made the charcoal that grown-up people used as medicine, or as fuel much better than ordinary wood, or for special uses in working iron.

One of the men gave me a little bit of charcoal, and told me that it could not do me any harm unless I bolted it at one go; and he was sure I was a young gentleman who wouldn't do that.

I was proud of the gift, and nibbled it on the way home. I rather liked the queer black crunch of it, but this blackened my lips and chin, and caused the confiscation of the treasure.

I never saw charcoal-burners elsewhere and count myself lucky to have seen these.

Down the slope, at the brink or border of the land

known to me, was a small hollow of wildness, overgrown with jungle, the source of yet another abundant spring. It was rich with growth and with blossom, but to our expert eyes seemed choked by its own over-vitality, and to be in need of a setting-free.

We debated what would be found, if the jungle were cut, and the cleansing gush set free. I was inclined to think that gold would be laid bare in heavy gold-dust, 'to be recognized at once by its great weight'.

At that time, diamonds were being found in parts of Africa, and an opposition party stood out for diamonds. This I could not agree to. It was well known, I said, that diamonds were found in blue clay, never in a red clay like ours.

This changed the question to whether there was any blue clay anywhere near us. This, we agreed, settled our chance of diamonds: the local clays were red, save in one valley to the south-east where it was a very pale adhesive yellow. We decided that both gold and diamonds were not to be found locally. The main wealth of our clay went into corn, cattle and roses. One garden of these last was close to us at that spot, and famous through that land of roses for a beauty, each June, beyond all telling by tongue.

Once, as we wandered home by the fields from that choked spring, we found a cowman, who had just driven into the field a herd of Hereford cattle. These are big upstanding beasts, red in frame, and yet white-faced. 'Yes,' this cowman said, 'and the most dangerous beasts in all Nature. With other cattle, one, perhaps, will come and toss you, but if one of these comes at you all will come.'

I cannot tell you what years of terror this friendly warning gave me. Long afterwards, I read in an American paper: 'Ananias is dead, but his spirit liveth.'

25

May Hill

I WAS never at nor very near to May Hill in those early years, but I thought of it often, and was glad of a sight of it.

This sight was rather rarely vouchsafed to me, for I did not often go where it could be easily seen.

The hill, I suppose, would be about seven miles from us, and at that distance it gave to us, on any clear day, a most vivid image of a man ploughing with a yoked team. No one could be in any doubt that at the top of the hill, facing the distant Severn (due south), a giant ploughman drove a team that never got any further.

The grown-up observer knew that the ploughman, the plough and the team were distant trees, but the little child thought that they were real ploughing figures, and giant figures. I know that they produced on myself an impression of enormous size, splendour and reality.

What if those figures were to come down and command men to do their bidding and bear a hand at ploughing the hill?

The impression that those giant figures were real, yet beneficent, was most real to me, and I could not doubt it for several early years.

I heard some talk about May Hill, as about Marcle Hill and Woolhope, that there was 'a geological fault or faults there' that made (rather frequently) slight earth tremors in those parts.

Then, in addition to the fault or faults, which gave one just cause for uneasiness, there had been a battle on May Hill in the Civil War, and I heard that one could still grub up small cannon-balls there. We had some of these, by the way, three or four, weighing about a pound apiece. I heard that one could scrape up such balls by the dozen, but I never learned where the battle had been nor when it had happened. I never added to our store of cannon-balls, and lost those that we had by using them as bowls in some improvised game with them.

I heard, too, that on May Hill there was a gallows, a real gallows, where men had been hanged and also gibbeted, and that under the gibbet you could grub up bits of old highwaymen.

This was true enough, however dreadful, and long afterwards I saw the remains of it: a stout timber stock, so beset with nails of a peculiar make that it could not be readily sawn asunder.

I was often on May Hill at odd times much later in life and saw the ruins of the ploughing figure and his team. They were good-sized fir trees coming to ruin and decay; storms had wrecked the wonder of their pose, that once had so moved and awed me on the road to Gloucester going down to the larches on Bullen Bank.

26

Flood Water

THERE is a stirring Australian word for any man shrewd at foretelling weather. Such a man is called 'skywonky'. It is hard to be skywonky, and people should begin early in life to become so in time.

For a time, I was reasonably skywonky, but, like other perfections, it is one that seldom lasts; but I began by watching the weather from our western windows.

First I watched for the visible sign of the Black Mountains away in Wales. Then, when the foretold rain had fallen, I looked out across the canal to see if a lot of rain had fallen. If the valley below the hills showed green, not much had fallen, but if the valley showed as a reddish smudge, then, beyond all doubt the Leddon was out, and we could go out to gloat at the mess, and scare ourselves with the power displayed.

Away we went, in the clearing gusts and the rising barometer; and in field after field we would see the spouting of springs and hear the gush in the ditches.

We did not linger at these lesser signs; we were for the real thing, a good half-mile from home just beyond the New Mills at the bridge over the Leddon.

The bridge itself was a sight to see, and the sight was one to be laid well to heart, for its parapet bore a metal plate, that told the traveller that anyone found damaging the bridge would be liable on conviction to be transported for seven years.

That was something to bear in mind, for our elders had told us that 'transported' meant being put into a transport, sailed to Australia, and having no birthdays, and very likely no Christmas either. Our one hope was in the words 'on conviction'; we might not be convicted.

(As a matter of fact, this transportation business had been ended more than thirty years before.)

But coming to the bridge, we went to the warning parapet, leaned upon it lightly, and surveyed the wonder.

It was, and is, a terrifying joy to look at flood.

The watcher saw the river coming round a bend at him, with a kind of a snarl, all red and wrinkled and evil. Nothing, it seemed, could withstand its rush. On its swirl came its bits of straw, sticks and leaves, all coming along full-tilt for the bridge we leaned on.

The mouth of the bridge was under water. One would see a log swirling down in the current smite the brickwork and be sucked under one's feet out of sight. Then authority would say, 'There now, you see where you would have been if you had been in the water.'

We could not see, alas, for the log so sucked down did not re-emerge on the other side of the bridge where we could see it.

The hills that border the valley, swiftly discharge the rain that falls; the floods rush down and are soon gone there. I never heard of farmstock lost in flood, nor saw a drowned mole nor rabbit.

All people dwelling near those parts knew what to expect in heavy rains, and knew that the roads were safe, and the fields dangerous.

79

27

Early Reading

LIFE itself is joy enough for many children, it is so full of new experience. It is strange later in life to think that reading must have been at one time a new experience, as vivid as life itself, being the life of every rainy day.

I cannot feel thus about my early reading. I did not begin to live for the joys of reading until some months after life itself as described in these pages ceased for me; but I had some fun out of books, now and then, quite early on.

I know that I found an early pleasure in some of the shorter poems of Milton; that I tried to read *Twelfth Night*, and had to give it up, but that I found much pleasure in Longfellow, some lyrics of Tennyson, some few poems of Adam Lindsay Gordon, and some of the stories of *The Ingoldsby Legends*, though these last were apt to become very terrible as twilight fell.

In some educational book for the young, a Reader for some tender age such as mine, I found a dreadful tale of a little child carried away by an eagle. There were illustrations to this tale that helped the imagination to reconstruct the event. The child had been taken to the fields by the working mother, and left, as such children were, wrapped up in woollens under a hedge, just as I had seen in the fields.

The eagle had come down, like the Assyrian in the poem, his cohorts (I supposed) gleaming with purple and gold, for was he not a golden eagle?

But all is not gold that glitters: this bird was thoroughly bad: he came, he saw, and he pounced; and there came a terrible and very skilful small engraving of him sailing westward with the babe in his claws. This was at the foot of a page which had letterpress upon it: such letterpress describing the anguish of the mother to see her son thus translated, and her frenzied effort to salve her babe.

I think it ended happily: it must have; but I cannot remember how, nor can I imagine how. The eagle had a good start, and could go the shortest way to his eyrie. The mother had to leave her work and call men to help, and then run with them to get to the eyrie before the great beak and talons had torn her darling to the panting open beaks of the eaglets.

I pictured at least six eaglets with open beaks and supposed that each would at once sample the child, with a bony beak and shrill ejaculations of joy. This part of the tale was like a real experience to me.

There was a rocky torn gash in the valley of the railway, above the tunnel. This showed the kind of place up which the mother, and the braves with her, had to hurry.

What happened I cannot now recollect; perhaps I could never dare to read it, and was told that all was well, as I feel sure it was in the end.

I was assured that these things no longer happened in England, but may have happened once, and no doubt might happen in less happy lands, if people were so careless as to leave a child under the hedge.

In this case with a golden eagle, the child was saved;

but there was another child, in another Reader, who was not saved, or seemed not to be saved to an impetuous king, with results appalling to a young heart.

This was the shocking story of the too-faithful Gelert, whose tomb could still be seen in North Wales, in the Snowdon district. In the memory of the too-faithful Gelert many children must have wept many pints of useless tears.

The tale was told by Southey in a ballad often printed in Readers for the young.

The too-impetuous king went hunting, leaving his little prince in his cradle guarded by a hound called Gelert.

The doors seemed to have been left open, for when the king returned from the hunt the palace was topsyturvy, with splashes of blood everywhere, the cradle upside-down, no little prince anywhere, and Gelert all spangled with gore yet seemingly satisfied.

Seeing this, the king rashly, but poetically exclaimed: 'Monster, thou hast devoured my child,' and at once slew Gelert, without further search.

A moment later, he learned that the prince was safe; that a wolf had attacked the prince, that Gelert had attacked and killed the wolf, but had not been able to put the child back into his cradle.

The king had bitterly repented his hurry; and given Gelert a tomb of splendour.

This piteous tale is wept over by most of the children who hear it. It was ever a most piteous tale to me. I know not how to describe my grief that the doors had not been locked and bolted and that the king had not waited for just one minute more. I am glad to think that another tale in verse by Southey gave me intense delight. I found this tale also in a Reader for the young. It was the tale 'King John and the Abbot'.

Southey has been a favourite storyteller to many millions of children. I owe to him the joy of the ballad of the 'Inchcape Rock', which I once knew by heart, and the matchless story, the faultless story (for children) of the 'Three Bears', a prose tale, which I read in a separate volume.

In the early 1880s many illustrated books, in prose and verse, were published in each year for the multitudes of children then beginning to read.

Of these I remember a wonderful book illustrated, I believe, by Walter Crane; a poem describing the fate of a much too talkative child, called 'Chattering Jack'. Another book, less well-illustrated, and less attractive in some ways, was of deep delight to myself. This was a poetical retelling of the truly great story of Christ, *The Man Born to be King*, one of those Deeds of the Romans that have a more ancient ancestry and belong to all time.

The tale of 'Chattering Jack' is an account of what happened to a child whose talk became a nuisance to all hands. He was translated suddenly to a nest of birds high up in a tree till he learned to be less of a pest. The illustrations to this book are better than the verse, though the verse has light and skilful movement. Among the illustrations are some very remarkable studies of the middle-class domestic scene.

The story *The Man Born to be King* is a work of much perfection; and this version of it was by a clever woman, a skilled nineteenth-century writer for the young, who must have given great pleasure to many thousands of children with this and her many other books. She opened to me a door into a great world of romance; her version gave me the first glimpse of that world. That has remained with me, as a guide and as a marvel for over eighty years.

Among the poems which meant much to me was an unusual poem by Miss Adeline Sergeant, which was printed in the magazine *Good Words* for 1882, with four illustrations by Irving Montague. I read it first at the end of 1882, and remember much of it to this day. It was a simple narrative much felt, and based (seemingly) upon something that may have happened in the then recent war in Afghanistan. It was called 'A Friend', and the illustrations represented English cavalry in foreign surroundings on active service.

I believed, then, that the event had happened.

Both the poem and its illustrations meant very much to me in my childhood. I see, now, that in those early days my longing for poetry was recognized, and not only permitted, but thoughtfully fostered and encouraged.

No word was said to me, but the fostering and encouragement were there; and poetry of simple kinds was there in abundance to delight me. The simple kinds were often of rare quality; among them were some of the best of Shakespeare, of Milton, and of then living masters, including Tennyson.

I have been asked, if any of my early reading turned me to the sea.

I was the third child in the family, and some of the books at hand were those given at past birthdays and Christmases to my elders.

Among these were several sea books, which I read with pleasure, such as the prose book *True Blue,* by a well-known writer for boys; a well-illustrated smaller book said to be by an old sailor called Grandpa Ben; and a copy of the ballad 'A ship, a ship, a-sailing', with coloured illustrations showing her crew of mice and her captain, a duck. I can remember no other book about the sea that came into my hands then, except one or two old volumes of *Punch* with ballads (two, I think) about whaling. These were clever arrangements of older originals, written and illustrated by G. Du Maurier.

I can only remember one marine publication that was altogether my own. This was a big printed red handkerchief showing that old wonder of the sea, the *Great Eastern*.

Long afterwards I saw the hull of that ship being slowly broken-up on the New Ferry sands on the Cheshire Mersey shore.

I have mentioned the books that I most dearly remember from those early years, some of them very early. There must have been many others, for I was always reading when I had the chance, but they have gone from memory.

The delightful works of Randolph Caldecott were known to me in those years, but were not, then, as dear to me as they became later. Few can have loved them more than I during the next few years.

I was a reader of old yearly numbers of *Little Folks* as well as of *Punch*. From the *Punch* volumes I became very familiar with Du Maurier's early work, and admired it intensely. It is his mockery of the Pre-Raphaelite Brotherhood that I most enjoyed, not knowing, nor suspecting then, that he was mocking what so thrilled my being.

I had two prose books of splendour, that I never tired of: a child's edition of *Robinson Crusoe*, and a book reprinted from Bell's *Life in London*, *The Australians in*

England, 1882. These I read in, and through, till they fell to pieces (or were suppressed). To this day the names Spofforth and H. H. Massie are names from the heart of Fairyland.

The year 1882 brought a great Australian team to England. It was the team that beat an all-England eleven at the Oval by seven runs in one of the great games still remembered.

The book that I so read and enjoyed was by Mr C. F. Pardon, who followed the entire tour and recorded every game with a delight and an interest that made his readers feel that they saw each unusual ball in the match, and what happened to it.

He followed the fortunes of another Australian eleven two years later, 1884. I had the book of that tour also, reprinted from Bell's *Life in London*. It was a less wonderful team than that of Spofforth's great year of 1882. It may be that Mr Pardon was less stirred by it. I never could care for it as I cared for its predecessor; but I can read it with pleasure still.

Quite recently I re-read both books with the ghosts of my old delight again reminding me. They are books well worth the reading and re-reading. They are remarkable also as sporting journalism by one who attended every match of the tour, and seems not to have missed one ball of the day's play, nor to have forgotten what each ball did.

Spofforth's great success came in 1882. On a chilly horrible day at the Oval Spofforth had said 'It can be done', and had then gone out to stop the English eleven from making eighty-five runs to win. By the help of Boyle and the others, they made only seventy-eight runs and English cricket was supposed to have burnt to ashes, though this lament has been proved to have been premature.

Long, long after that event, I knew an Australian who had helped to carry Spofforth in triumph to the pavilion when the game ended.

Once, too, long since, I spoke with one of the English team who, for some glorious minutes, made the issue hopeful for us.

From my memories of those first years, which ended when I was about six years and eight months old, I can extract some half-memories of two books that I could not understand, but yet felt to be strangely beautiful and inspired. One described the death of a boy, the other the courage of a soul in shipwreck.

I have thought of both these ghostly memories ever since, but not knowing what they were. Of death and shipwreck I was soon to know plenty.

For many years, I have thought of these early readings, and my enjoyment of them. What greater happiness is there in life

'Than to enjoy delight with liberty?'

I have come to see that there is no greater delight and that my delight was due to one human will, enlightened and generous beyond most, who could not be thanked then, for the child knew nothing of the gift, and so was not thanked at all. Death and shipwreck did their worst and had their day, but the gift of that early reading was alive in me, despite all shipwreck and death, which are parts of this scheme of things, in any case, and give releases and a justice, wise and unfailing.

Certain matters were very certain to me, in those early days; the certainty that I had lived before and should live again; the certainty of spiritual powers ever ready to help bright human endeavour; the certainty that the individual life follows a law from of old, the law of his being, and must obey that law with all that is good in him, and achieve what is good in him, or fail.

28

Piping Down

IT is time now, to pipe down and coil up.

All these matters happened more than eighty years ago, in an England with half her present population, filling a great place in the world though with sad insufficiencies.

One could hardly enter a town without seeing a drunken man or woman; children in rags, or in clothes sewn onto their bodies, children barefooted in frost; men unable to read or write; men marked with small-pox, and many young men getting out of England to begin elsewhere at all costs.

All these things we saw afflicting a kind, great, religious people, so great in their goodness, and their goodness so sorely tried.

Eighty years have brought such change as even a generous heart could scarcely have expected or even hoped; and here we are now, like Shakespeare, in some doubt saying, 'What's to come is still unsure.'

To most of us, it seems very unsure, but then, it always has been; and we, who have seen great changes, must have great hopes.

'Hope is a jewel,' somebody said. But Hope is not stolen, like so many jewels. Hope is a thing given, so that a more lovely thing can be.

Epilogue

Such is the living bread allowed,
(Should Fortune warrant), till a share
Rends all to tatters under cloud
With wrack and ruin everywhere,
As other fortune falls,
And buds are beaten bare.

In the unseen, in the unknown,
About us, planning, seeing, wise,
The Helpers comfort the alone
Through all that destinies devise.
Though waterless, in sand,
The buds break, being sown.

The Hopes that kindle man are true
The thought for others has reward,
Unseen, it makes the world anew,
Till loss regretted is restored,
And in man's darkest soul
The voiceless plea of love is harkened to.